Dyslexia Wonders

Dyslexia can help you Succeed

People with Dyslexia frequently enjoy above average skills including the ability to look at things differently and they are frequently artistically gifted. Dyslexia is not a sign of stupidity, ignorance, laziness or inferiority. The greatest barrier to success is mindset. The lack of confidence that comes from the frustration of not doing well in our school system can hinder progress. Dyslexia is easier when we believe we can.

Some of our more famous successful dyslexics include:

Richard Branson – Entrepreneur, Virgin brand of over 360 companies

Steven Spielberg – Film producer of many brilliant movies

Henry Winkler – Actor, director and producer

Steve Jobs – Founder of Apple Computers

Robin Williams – Actor and comedian

Suzanne Somers – Actress and entrepreneur

Thomas Edison – Inventor of the light bulb and held 1,093 patents

Whoopi Goldberg – Actress. comedian and singer

Cher – Actress and singer

Tom Cruise- Actor and producer

Jennifer Smith – Author, singer, speaker

Albert Einstein – Genius, great thinker and super intelligent

Charles Schwab – A billionaire financier and founder of Charles Schwab

Magic Johnson – Basketball Legend

Jay Leno – Comedian, late night TV host

John F. Kennedy – 35th President of the United States

Mohammad Ali – Olympic light heavyweight boxing champion

Walt Disney – Film producer, director, founder of Disney Land

General George Patton – U.S. Army General

Babe Ruth – Greatest of all baseball players

Leonardo DaVinci - Artist

Orlando Bloom - Actor

Henry Ford- Founder of Ford Company

Ted Turner- founder of CNN

Winston Churchill-Former Prime Minister of the UK

Find your Leadership skills within your dyslexia

Praise for *Dyslexia Wonders*

"This book is terrific!!!! I am supposed to be planning my classes for second semester but I decided that I would read it. I have read every word.

I knew that you had had educational struggles, Jennifer, but I had no idea what you had been going through. This book is very clearly written for the layperson (so that they can help their children) and for possible dyslexics-------and very-powerfully and -inspirationally written. The book's content and organization are superb."

Andrea Splittberger-Rosen Ph.D
http://www.uwsp.edu/music/people/faculty/arosen.aspx

"Awesome book, Jennifer! Thanks for helping us all understand what it is like to have dyslexia. I can hardly wait to share your book when it comes out with other dyslexics and teachers I know."

Garry Reenders
International Dyslexia Association
Board Member, Michigan

"An absolute joy to read"
Bonnie May Fowler

Dyslexia Wonders

~

Understanding the Daily Life of a Dyslexic from a Child's Point of View

~

Jennifer Smith

New York

Dyslexia Wonders
Understanding the Daily Life of a Dyslexic
From a Child's Point of View

ISBN 978-1-60037-634-4

Library of Congress Control Number: 2009927108

MORGAN · JAMES
THE ENTREPRENEURIAL PUBLISHER
Morgan James Publishing, LLC
1225 Franklin Ave., STE 325
Garden City, NY 11530-1693
Toll Free 800-485-4943
www.MorganJamesPublishing.com

In an effort to support local communities, raise awareness and funds, Morgan James Publishing donates one percent of all book sales for the life of each book to Habitat for Humanity. Get involved today, visit www.HelpHabitatForHumanity.org.

Giving Back

A big thank you to the Grand Rapids Learning
Center for Children, for helping me reach
my potential in reading and writing and for
making the future brighter for me.

I couldn't have done it without you
and your support.

I'm going to give back a percentage of the profits
from this book to help children with Dyslexia.

Learn more about my mission and how
you can help provide tutoring and special
events for kids who have Dyslexia.

"I want it said of me by those who knew me
best that I always plucked a thistle and planted
a flower where I thought a flower would grow"

Abraham Lincoln

Acknowledgements

Mary Moore, my all-around helper in writing, editing (again, and again, and again) I wouldn't have gotten this book done without you.

Thanks to everyone who helped proof read and edit the book. Thanks to my Mother, Anita Smith who was the spark plug behind this project.

The Artist

My special thanks to the Illustrator, Allison Witte. She is an amazing young artist and I am thankful for her talent. Her contribution to my book has been a labor of love and friendship and I thank her for taking the time to create the illustrations in the book.

Allie and I had got caught passing a note in class. We silently blamed the note-passing on a little creature called the 'Note-Mite'. Thus was born the Monster File. Allie has a vivid imagination and created monsters to help and hinder in every creek and cranny of our school. Check out the Monster File at www.dyslexiawonders.com/monster

God, my ever-present friend and protector. You are awesome indeed.

Special Thanks

To my wonderful parents and my very special grandparents: You have been so supportive. I love you all.

To Nana and Papa, who always believed in me and would sometimes drive me to tutoring.

To my brothers, Brian and Brad: You helped develop within me the courage to stand up for myself, to love who I am, and to continue to have a sense of humor.

To my best friend, Ryah, who encouraged me to always be myself, to be real, and to believe in myself.

Also to my tutor, Jeanne, who gave her time, effort, and patience through the many years.

Thanks to Nina for admitting me into the Center even though she was hesitant because my mom had to drive me over an hour each way two times a week. The drive made me appreciate what the Center did for me a little more. I am very glad to have been a part of her life and that she decided to accept me into the program.

Thank you all!

Contents

Chapter 1
Discovering Dyslexia

"Success is the sum of many small efforts."
Robert J Collier

What you are about to read may be the story of people you know and love, but it happens to be my story as well.

My grandfather was worried because at the age of five, I still could not sing the ABC song. At six, I could sometimes sing it, and when I was seven, I knew it by heart, even though I could not recite the ABCs in order. At eight years old, I impressed my worried grandfather by singing the ABC song backwards, but what he did not know was that I could not say or write the ABCs on a consistent basis. I was able to sing the ABCs backwards because I had memorized the ABC song backwards. I could not even read the easy Dr. Seuss books.

Because I was homeschooled, I had the flexibility of trying a variety of school programs and curriculums, as well as of receiving individual instruction and tutoring. My two brothers had both been in the public school system through their early elementary years, and neither had this level of difficulty learning to read.

When I was five and again when I was six, my mom took me to the doctor to see if she could make a diagnosis or if there was a test I could take to find out what could be wrong. The doctor told us not to worry; I was still young, and everyone learns to read at different times. She then said her favorite motivational line to me: "Jennifer, you are not stupid." Being the caring doctor that she was, she had told me that many times.

Awhile later, Mom took me to the public school and asked if I could be tested, only to find that testing wasn't done until students were in fourth grade. This was very disappointing to me as I was only a third grader and would have to wait another whole year.

If not being able to learn the ABCs wasn't bad enough, I also had trouble with the letter names and sounds. The way I learned my phone number was by Mom making up a song and then singing it over and over and over until it was stamped into my brain. I can still sing my old phone number and probably will when I am eighty years old!

Learning to tie my shoes was another major feat. I loved shoes with Velcro, but what I really wanted were those flashy sneakers that would light up when you walked, and I just had to have them. But Mom refused to buy me a combination of Velcro and the light-up shoes—she made me choose. In order to get the ones I wanted so badly, I knew I would have to somehow, someway learn to tie my shoelaces. With the help of my brothers, I finally did, and I didn't even care that I used the "baby" version, by making two rabbit ears, crossing them over each other and through the rabbit hole. I can still remember the day Mom took me shopping for those lovely, bright pink, light-up shoes. I was eight years old. It was one of the happiest days of my life. Afterwards, Dad made a board for me to carry around that showed each step of how to tie, and he worked with me for long periods of time, too. When I was finally able to tie in "adult style," we celebrated together with an ice cream.

And all the while I continued to stumble over the pesky alphabet. Because I'd had numerous ear infections as an infant, my ears and eyes were checked by a pediatric specialist to make sure nothing was wrong and interfering with my ability to learn. I was almost disappointed when he gave me a clean bill of health and assured me they were fine and normal.

When I was eight years old, I began attending classes at a homeschool center about an hour away that offered structured classes once a week. I went mainly because it offered the more advanced classes that my brothers needed, such as algebra II, physics, and advanced composition. I enrolled in choir, reading comprehension, art, and keyboarding.

The most terrible class I took was reading comprehension because I was the only one in my age group who couldn't read. To make matters worse, each week we had to read an entire book out loud in front of the class. In order to avoid embarrassment, I did what any other kid would do; I faked it. A week ahead of time, I selected a book with a minimal amount of words and took the book home for Mom to read to me. Over and over and over she read out loud until I memorized the whole thing, all the while thinking she was helping me comprehend the content. When it was my turn to read aloud in front of the class, I sounded like I was reading perfectly. No one knew that in reality I was not reading but was reciting from memory.

Trying to actually read the books was impossible. The words were as if they were Chinese. Not only did they appear foreign to me but also fuzzy. As if the words were moving and jumbled up all at the same time.

But even though I memorized books quite often, I still felt that my memorization skills were inadequate. At the library, I checked out more videos and tapes than I did books and listened to stories such as *Where the Red Fern Grows, The Secret Garden*, the Harry Potter books, and *Matilda*. Then I created chants, sang songs, and even stood on my head in an effort to memorize. One reason I felt so inadequate was that my brother Brad was in a Bible quiz program and he could memorize entire chapters of the Bible faster than I could memorize a twenty-word book. Because I really, really wanted to read, I took to learning any way I could.

Computer keyboarding class was also extremely difficult. When we had to copy paragraphs directly from a book, my work was not legible. I simply could not read the letters and words, decipher them in my brain, and type them out. But when we typed what the teacher read out loud, not only was my work above average in accuracy, I was one of her fastest typists!

One day after class, the instructor pulled Mom aside and told her about the problems I was having. She said that my keyboarding skills were quite amazing when the words were spoken out loud, yet fell dramatically when read from paper. She explained that this was common in individuals with dyslexia and then added,

> *"If I ever met anyone who has dyslexia, it is your daughter. You need to have her tested and have it done now!"*

"If I ever met anyone who has dyslexia, it is your daughter. You need to have her tested and have it done now!"

She handed brochures to Mom and me and told us of a place where her own son was going to treat his dyslexia. Perhaps, she said, they might be able to help me.

Mom wasted no time in calling the director of the program, Nina, who was very helpful and nice and answered all of our questions. Soon afterwards, I went to a psychologist to be tested, and the results confirmed what my teacher had thought: I had dyslexia. With this diagnosis I was accepted into the program.

Unfortunately, there was a one-year waiting list to get into the program, and the program was one hour from home. Mom researched closer alternatives only to learn they were very expensive. She said she couldn't stand by and not help me for a whole year, so she found a tutor who specialized in learning-challenged kids to help me until I could get in. But because the tutor did not understand how I processed information, this was not a good program for me ... but I certainly did love the candy I received for completing the homework!

And finally, after what seemed to be a very long year, a tutor was available for me at the Children's Learning Center.

I remember setting foot in that building for the very first time. The ceilings were tall, and there was a large grandfather clock directly inside the entryway. I was frightened; I thought I was going to get lost in the huge building. I was also afraid everyone would judge me too quickly. Thankfully, I was wrong. The people there were wonderful, so kind and friendly, especially my teacher, Jeanne, who was always very patient and understanding. In the three years I was there, I got to know her very well.

After attending the Learning Center for two weeks, I took another trip to the library and that time left with fewer videos and more books than usual. That was a major step for me. Several weeks later, I checked out only one video and four books. Soon after that, I borrowed five books and no videos. As my reading skills improved, so did my love for books, and I began to look forward to the challenge of more difficult levels.

Something that helped my reading skills improve was a process that they taught me at the Children's Learning Center that was called "pounding." You take your hand and pat your leg or your arm, kind of like the syllables are being pounded into your brain. It helped me memorize faster, because it made the words into rhythms. Each word had its own unique rhythm. When you put the words with the right rhythm you knew if it was right or wrong. I still use this method in high school today.

By now I was reading at home on my own as well as with my tutor, Jeanne, and we ended each session by reading a book together. She would have me read it aloud, and if I stumbled on a word, she would tell me the meaning and then help me sound it out. Soon she didn't have to help me at all because I learned to figure out the words and how they sounded.

While attending the Children's Learning Center, I also enrolled in a co-op school for homeschoolers. There I took a number of classes, including English, spelling, and science, and I enjoyed most of them, especially PE, which was held at the end of the day. It felt good to stretch my legs after sitting for so long.

But even though I loved most of my classes, I hated English, which happened to be taught by my best friend's mother. She was very demanding and assigned a great deal of writing homework, and needless to say, she did not go easy on me just because I was her daughter's best friend. Instead, she held the entire class to a very high standard. Many homeschool teachers raise the bar for their students, and I've always wondered if it is because they believe the students need this in order to succeed in today's world or if they like having their students perform on a higher academic plane than those who attend public school.

She doled out an excessive amount of homework, and it was extremely stressful for me to keep up. Even though I was learning to overcome dyslexia, it was a slow process, and I still had a long way to go. Often, Mom encouraged me to rewrite my homework because my spelling and handwriting skills were so poor and my writing, illegible. I remember spending hours and hours every day working on those English homework assignments: it was difficult, frustrating, and not at all enjoyable!

My teacher didn't understand dyslexia; she didn't understand that it affected my ability to complete the homework in what would otherwise be a reasonable amount of time. Even though I spent hours every night just doing my English and I tried my best, she would not accept any reason for my work not being done to her satisfaction. I had not been in the Grand Rapids tutoring program very long and still had a lot of trouble successfully completing my homework assignments. Every week I came home crying about English because I just didn't get it. Even though it was only creative writing, I felt it was too advanced for me.

One day we were given the assignment of writing a story using pictures we had drawn earlier; then later the same day, we were to stand at a podium in front of the classroom and present the story orally. I was horrified. My story was about a volleyball game between sea animals, and while my pictures were totally acceptable—and actually rather cute—I was in no way ready to speak in front of my peers, much less able to read to them. My reading skills were still severely lacking, and I was not ready for that.

When it came time for me to make my presentation that afternoon, I trembled and shook so badly that not only could I not read what I'd written because of the dyslexia, I couldn't see what was on the papers because they were shaking so badly in my hands! I sure handed the kids who teased me a lot of ammunition that day. During PE class I was taunted about my poor performance and was called "Seizure" for the rest of the day.

Had I been given the assignment with time to practice (memorize) at home, I knew I would have done a good job. However, I left school that day humiliated and never wanted to participate publicly again.

After attending one semester at this co-op, I refused to take classes from that teacher again. I hadn't learned anything because I couldn't understand the way she taught. All I did during that class was cry out of frustration. Mom had tried to intervene during the semester on behalf of all the kids with academic learning challenges, and a few other parents went into the classroom and offered their assistance as well.

The parents were all trying to help those students avoid falling further behind. Although this did help somewhat, I felt singled out and different from the other kids in the class. Instead of learning the class material, I spent a lot of energy worrying about keeping up and wondering if the other kids were going to make fun of me after class.

It did not even help when I found out that the advanced kids were also having difficulty dealing with the amount of homework for the class.

At ten years old, I finally was able to read at a basic level, but by then I had been teased relentlessly by many, including both of my brothers. Whether or not it was true, it sure seemed like my brothers were waiting for me to fail again. They enjoyed teasing me, and I could normally give it right back. I would cringe at the thought of walking past my brothers when I felt too vulnerable to deal with their friendly banter. Of course I never let them know how painful the teasing was, but when it went too far and I could no longer handle feeling stupid, I hibernated in my room and cried myself to sleep. And our parents didn't know because my brothers and I went out of our way to make sure they didn't see and hear what was said "in friendly brotherly and sisterly love." I felt a lot of pressure, and I only made it harder on myself since even I thought I was stupid and would never learn to read.

I thought I was stupid and would never learn to read.

My discouragement came to a head when I learned that my cousin, who is four years younger than me, could read much faster and more clearly than I could. That's when I decided to take more drastic actions and bring my reading to a whole new level. I was finally ready—really ready—to get help with my reading problem. I wanted to read, and I wanted to read now! I knew how important it was, and I knew that in order to get the kind of education I wanted, I would have to comprehend what I was learning.

To be honest, because of my cousin, I realized time was not on my side. I knew that I needed to go deep within myself to figure out what was wrong with my brain. I finally decided that I would discipline myself like a Marine. A new will began to rise within me! I was determined to not let my age or all the teasing or anything else discourage me. I decided that my strong will and outgoing personality were what would help me through this ordeal—not the avoidance of reading among my peers! My mindset was all the difference that it took to make me try my best.

> *My mindset was all the difference that it took to make me try my best.*

When I first began attending the Children's Learning Center, my tutor and I began with books that were five pages long. When I left the Center three years later, we were in the middle of a two-hundred-page chapter book. Together, Jeanne and I had done the unthinkable by changing the way I saw letters and comprehended words. Amazing transformations had been taking place in my life!

It makes me disappointed when I tell someone my own age that I have dyslexia and they ask, "What is dyslexia?"

Sadly, it is a common occurrence to hear that question, but it gives me the chance to educate someone in a positive way. I usually reply that a dyslexic has many talents. One of mine is that I am a person who can read and write backwards, and when you hold my handwriting up to the mirror it shows up in the correct format.

Generally speaking, dyslexics are creative and musically inclined. In my case, I've always loved to draw and paint, mainly fashion designs. Mom often went to the arts and crafts store and, using half-off coupons, would purchase canvases of all sizes for me. I've painted everything from a very tiny picture to one that covers an entire wall of my room. Many of my paintings have been given away as Christmas and thank-you gifts. And when I get tired of a particular painting, I simply paint a brand new masterpiece right over the top! Painting helps me de-stress and enjoy my world more.

As for music, I've always loved to sing and wanted to join the church choir, but I didn't know if my voice was special enough. When I heard about an upcoming competition, I asked the program organizer, Mrs. Wong, if I could compete, and she said I could but that I would need someone to play the piano for me. Then I asked if she would help me and she agreed! Mom was there to cheer me on and videotape my competition, and I was thrilled to place in the top ten. There were over thirty girls competing, all of whom had received years of professional voice lessons. Although I did not win, the judges gave me some very encouraging feedback, and after that, I took about ten voice lessons from a teacher at the local community college.

Another frequently asked question is, "What does it feel like to be a dyslexic?" It's hard to describe, but I would say that it's like being in a box and screaming to get out. But no matter what you do, you can't. You struggle and struggle to escape, but you're trapped. And every time it seems like you're almost out, you fall back in. Eventually you get so frustrated that you want to quit altogether. You want to read, but you just can't. But when you start thinking outside the box, the challenge that once stood before you as a great threat, only seems like an empty box. You look at it with new eyes and a new perspective. The world makes more sense and seems less hopeless. It makes you actually start to look forward to things that you never used to. Basically you jump up and down and scream your head off, saying, "I did it! I did it! I learned how to read!" You walk away feeling so proud of yourself, and others feel proud of you, too. When everything seems to fall into place, it gets easier. When that happened to me, I wanted to read all day long.

"Self- pity gets you nowhere. One must have the adventurous daring to accept oneself as a bundle of possibilities and undertake the most interesting game in the world making the most of one's best."

Richard Willard Armour

Chapter 2
Be There for Us

*"Pray that success will not come any faster
than you are able to endure it."*
Benjamin Nnamdi Azikiwe

For parents, it is often difficult to determine if a child is being disobedient or if he simply does not understand the instruction. I was very blessed to have been homeschooled and receive encouragement and support from my parents. I've known other children with learning challenges who were not so lucky.

Dyslexia is actually more common than one might think. If your child is bright but consistently struggles with his studies, ask yourself: is he truly giving his best effort, or is he just being lazy? Sadly, some parents do think that their child is slacking off and doesn't want to do the work. I have heard of many punishments for these children, whose only real crime was being born different in mind and learning styles.

Punishment is not going to solve a learning disability, and could instead dishearten the child even more. People with learning problems may resort to skipping homework because they don't know what to do, or perhaps they may just look at it blankly because to them it looks like gibberish. I've been there. Personally, I think that it is unfair to accuse us of disobeying.

If you want to help, then guide your child and walk with him in the right direction. If he does not have confidence in himself, your words will be lost. Instead of a pointless punishment, figure out a clever way to make him see the problem from a different angle. Hopefully, he will listen to what you have to say and want to figure out a solution, too. Is there a particular subject with which your child is struggling? Getting the teacher's advice and viewpoint might help you see the situation more clearly.

But remember that after you get help for your child, you must continue to be there for him, encouraging, helping, and guiding. In order for him to make progress, you as the parent need to know where to start, so that you can also help your child finish.

For a dyslexic, reading is a lifetime learning process, improved over time; it will not be "fixed" overnight. It's also very possible that your child won't read exceptionally well, or even be up to his own grade level, for two or three years after getting the appropriate help. When I was in the Children's Learning Center, it took three years for me to fully read and write at my own grade level. During the last year, I went from fifth-grade reading to eighth-grade reading, and I was actually only in sixth grade when I graduated from the Learning Center!

There are many ways to overcome dyslexia, and I will talk about those later. Right now, I just want to plead with you to just love your child. Be kind, caring, and encouraging. Give unconditional love and know he is not trying to misbehave. He is frustrated and embarrassed that he can't read; he feels as though he is different, like he is disappointing you.

Remember, for the dyslexic, learning to read is extremely hard. Most likely, it will take both you and your child's time and effort to do this. You, yourself, may even want to quit at some point, thinking it is a waste of time, but you must not. Neither of you can afford to quit; if you do, you're risking your child's entire future and everything that's been accomplished. It is so important to stay focused! He will need to be able to read and comprehend road signs when he's old enough to drive. He'll want to read the same literature that his friends are reading. And he'll be unhappy that he's so far behind everyone he knows. You should know that in order to really help your child, you will have to give up things you want to do in order to stick to the commitment that you make at the beginning of this fight.

Another thing that makes it extremely difficult for young dyslexics to learn is the cruelty they experience from peers. I was homeschooled, so it was easier for me; and it also helped that my schedule was flexible. And yet I still was taunted. It is very sad that children find it so difficult to cope with someone who is different.

So when it seems as though your child is disobeying with their reading and homework, it might simply be due to a learning disability. It will take both of you to be able to get up in the morning and say that today is a new day. All in all, you must decide how you want to handle the situation yourself, and let your child know that, through it all, you will be there for him.

Chapter 3
For Those Who Don't Know

"If your ship doesn't come in, swim out to it."
Jonathan Winters

This is for the parents, friends, and people at school who know someone with dyslexia. It's hard to understand what a person with dyslexia goes through and how he feels. But when someone doesn't know how to respond, he or she often will tease and taunt the dyslexic child and say terrible things that may seem meaningless but are, in reality, very hurtful and embarrassing.

For instance, my brother, who is very bright, thought that I was dumb and couldn't do anything, and he told me so. He teased me and said I was stupid. When a person hears those words more than once every day, he starts believing them. My spirit started to crumble, and I was beginning to lose any hope of being able to read.

My brother didn't know what I was going through, and his teasing caused me to believe that he thought of me as though I were nothing. In turn, I felt worse about myself, and the more he taunted me, the more difficult it became for me to learn. Please never say that dyslexics are stupid; it breaks their hearts. Instead, be an encourager and help by doing whatever you can. When someone offers help, as opposed to ridicule, it feels like somebody else actually cares, and in turn, that brings a feeling of hope.

I remember once attempting to read a book that was only five pages long. It took hours for me to finish, and even then it was because Mom sat with me all during that time. She repeated the alphabet and the sounds of each letter.

My brother Brad would also help by reading to me over and over. He even tape-recorded the more advanced books that my friends were reading so I could follow along with my finger. I knew he loved me and cared about me. He had no idea how much I hurt from his cruel words because we never took each other very seriously. Now I realize I should have gone to my parents and explained what my brother said to me and how it was affecting me.

My family has always been supportive of me through and through. I've always said that, no matter what happens, I will read and live my life to the best of my ability. And since then I have also tried to be an example to others, showing them that they should take a look at the people around them and take time to make a difference in their lives.

Math was another difficult subject, and my friends helped tremendously. My friend, Ryah, took a lot of time teaching me division. Because of the kindness and patience of my family, friends, and teachers, especially Jeanne, I've not been teased in many years. Now it's time for me to give back and help others who need me.

As a result of your helping those who have trouble learning, someday their lightbulbs will turn on so bright you'll think they're the sun! You could look back and say, "I was the one to help that person!" You'll get the exact same amount of pride in yourself that you gave to the person you helped.

Now you know how a lack of understanding can affect a dyslexic.

"Flatter me, and I may not believe you. Criticize me, and I may not like you, Ignore me, and I, may not forgive you. Encourage me, and I may not forget you."

Sir William Arthur

Chapter 4
Live Your Legacy Now

"Sow an act...reap a habit; Sow a habit...reap a character; Sow a character...reap a destiny."
George Dana Boardman

There were times during school when I would have to be on the quiz team. Members were expected to memorize random facts and quotes. But my memory was seldom able to retain anything. This just became another nightmare for me to deal with.

This was a common theme: I would be told that the letters *t-h-e* spelled "the." Some days I could grasp this, but on other days, I couldn't. It was frustrating to learn something and then have all that hard work go away because I couldn't remember.

It was usually the red words that I forgot. *Red words* are those, such as *the*, *one*, and *two*, which do not follow the regular spelling rules or patterns of the English language. Check out the list on my Web site, www.dyslexiawonders.com.

When I attended a tutoring center, the teacher would explain something to me, but I would forget it as soon as I left. It was so terribly frustrating. The only reason I kept up with the homework packets they gave me was that I was rewarded with candy. I never understood the homework packets, but I made it look like I did.

I never told this to my parents; they thought things were improving. I wish I had told the truth that I wasn't learning anything. Maybe they could have found a different tutor who would have helped me truly learn to read.

At the Children's Learning Center, I learned several sensory techniques to help me remember. One way was to hold out my arm and pat on it with my other hand as I spelled out a word, as though I was pounding the word right into my body. Another method was to write a word in the sand, which helped me visualize the word as well as feel it while writing. Also, I wrote red words with a felt marker in the color red, which helped me feel the shape of the letters as I said them aloud.

As I began understanding the English language, my self-confidence grew, and my memory started to kick in. I didn't mess up dates or appointments; I remembered what I was supposed to do on a particular day, what I had eaten earlier, and many other details that otherwise might seem trivial. An amazing thing started to take place: As I understood one thing, I began to understand many other things. Math, science, music, French, and other school subjects became easier. The pieces of the puzzle started to come together, and things started to make sense when I learned how to read.

I now know that as a dyslexic I should have learned Spanish as it is an easier foreign language to spell than French is. I stuck with French, and I am currently in my third year. I hope to be able to visit France and have an opportunity to use my French.

Before I knew I had the disability called dyslexia, I sulked around my home, thinking and planning ways to be able to read. But every plan I tried, failed. Mom bought every program available, and she was also saddened by my inability to grasp the concepts. And even though it seemed that every single curriculum failed, Mom still sought out more, and I kept trying.

I believe that for budgetary reasons the public schools were not interested in helping me, and private schools did not have the necessary resources. Both entities were leery of labeling me, indicating that it might hurt me down the road.

Even though I was homeschooled for most of my elementary and middle school years, I had the right to use the resources offered by the public school system. However, this did not make the system easier to maneuver. In fact having someone to be your advocate is sometimes necessary.

No matter what happened, I always said that there was no point to life if you did not try, so I never gave up hope. I would cry sometimes out of frustration when I got discouraged, but I never wanted to cry and give up. Once a person gives up hope, he'll be giving up a chance to be something great, for there is always a way to read. You know the old saying: "Where there's a will, there's a way."

> *Once a person gives up hope, he'll be giving up a chance to be something great.*

Anyone who has trouble reading, whether he is dyslexic or not, will always feel pressure about his reading skills. But take heart because there are programs available for every learning style you can think of. If you don't give up, you can handle yourself with such grace that you will succeed with flying colors. I guarantee it.

I can still hear the words that inspired me from my parents and grandparents. The words were, "You can grow up and do whatever you want to do." I took those words to heart and went through my learning programs determined to do what I dreamed of. I got through it even though my dreams have changed many times through the years. I still have the goal of doing whatever I want to. And now all I have to do is get through high school and college, get my dream job, and have fun living life.

Sounds pretty simple, doesn't it? Don't be fooled; it's very hard work and takes a lot of effort to accomplish what you dream. You have to fight for it if you truly want it.

I will always try, and I have learned to never give less than my best at whatever I do. There is always a way to learn, and you will be successful as long as you try your hardest and with the best attitude you can. You will prosper. As I said before, never give up hope because you can't afford to. There is always a way to learn to read. Even if it seems extremely dismal, you can accomplish your dreams if they mean enough to you.

You will build character by living in this way; and in the process, you'll live your legacy, your life. Your legacy will reflect your values. *Be strong and live your legacy now.*

Chapter 5
Special Gifts

"Such as are your habitual thoughts,
such also will be the character of your mind;
for the soul is dyed by the thoughts."
Marcus Aurelius Antoninus

Most people wake up in the morning believing that they're normal, that they are nothing special. I used to be one of those people. As I was looking in the mirror one day, I tried to figure out what made me different from everyone else. My mom always told me I was her angel from heaven. I wondered why God would send an angel who couldn't read and was slow to learn everything. To this day I don't know my multiplication tables, and I am a horrible speller. I believe my family loves me for who I am, normal or not.

While looking at my reflection in the mirror I realized that no one can truly call themselves normal. What is the definition of normal? Other than a setting on a clothes dryer, there really isn't one. We all have special gifts that appear at different times in our lives. We don't necessarily realize what our unique abilities are until they are pointed out. You can't realize what you have until you know it exists. This is what happened to me as a dyslexic.

Through the years, I have learned more and more about dyslexia. It isn't a curse but a blessing in disguise. For instance, I have discovered so many gifts inside of me, and I haven't even seen them all yet. I know that I am creative. Not only do I love music, but I'm good at it, too. There are so

> *What is the definition of normal?*
> *Other than a setting on a clothes dryer, there really isn't one.*

many gifts in everyone, both dyslexic and non-dyslexic. I have learned some very interesting facts through the years. I think you would enjoy learning about them, too.

I recently found out that dyslexics are more right-brain dominant than left, which means they have a tendency to be more artistic. For example, if a dyslexic looks at a flower, he doesn't just see the front of it; he sees the entire creation—the sides, the back, and the myriad of different colors.

Here's something else I found interesting: Many famous people have been discovered to have had dyslexia. Leonardo DaVinci was a dyslexic, but that's not so surprising because he was so creative and used his ability to be a great painter. There are a lot of wonderful gifts that people have put to great use in the past.

Albert Einstein was another of the great gifted inventors we have had with dyslexia. He was a genius at math and the mysteries of the universe. Another example is Thomas Edison, who, before he finally creating the light bulb, failed approximately ten thousand times! Nonetheless, he never gave up. And let's not forget Alexander Graham Bell, the brilliant inventor of the telephone.

Henry Winkler is an actor, director and producer who is most famous for his role as Arthur "Fonzie" Fonzarelli on the popular sitcom Happy Days. Henry has created a children's book series called Hank Zipzer, the world's greatest underachiever. Henry Winkler and his co-author share the struggles and triumphs of a resourceful elementary school student as he deals with the challenges that come with dyslexia. The stories are based on Henry Winkler's own experiences with dyslexia.

These men were given amazing gifts, which they used to aid the world and create so many absolutely ingenious inventions and artistic contributions. You see, there is more than one kind of gift. There are many more people with dyslexia who have gifts and have put them to good use. To add yourself to my list of dyslexics and tell me about your story, go to my Web site, www.dyslexiawonders.com.

Usually, dyslexics get so caught up in their reading disability that they don't realize the wonderful gifts they have, and instead they become consumed with their poor reading skills. If you have dyslexia, it may take you your entire life to discover your gifts and talents. But do not give up hope, for you will find a gift some day and use it in the manner that it was given for you to use. Everyone is given a special gift, so don't stop until you have discovered yours.

Chapter 6
You Are Not Alone

"No one can make you feel inferior without your consent."
Eleanor Roosevelt

When I learned that there were more people just like me struggling to read and that some of them were famous, it made me feel really good inside. I started doing better in my tutoring, and I made it known to the instructors that I had dyslexia. I also made it known that I had something in common with the great inventors of our time, something that I was really proud of. (Like I said, there is a list of names on my Web site.)

It isn't just me that this list has inspired. I showed the exact same list to a friend of my mom's, who showed it to her son, who has dyslexia. She said that, after he read the list of names, his spirits were brightened, and he became even more determined to read.

What inspired me to put the list on my Web site was that I knew it had brightened the spirits of others when they learned about these inventors. I hope that someone else will truly feel how wonderful it is to know that he or she is not the only one in the world going through this. I know I did.

You never should feel that you are going through something alone. You have your family and your friends to help along your difficult path, and many others have gone down this same road before you. Admittedly, there are some bumps and twists and turns along the way, but do not be discouraged. You will always have help

if you ask for it. The scripture goes, "Ask and you shall receive." I've always found that saying to be correct and very truthful. I mean, if I hadn't asked Mom to help me with my dyslexia and my mind-set in my time of need, I would probably not have written this book. If I hadn't asked I wouldn't be at the level I am now in my reading and schooling.

Mom was a real trooper. She never complained about driving me every Monday and Wednesday for three years to the Learning Center, forty-five minutes away—a grand total of 24,840 miles driven in order for me to learn! The 720 hours spent driving and attending the Children's Learning Center in downtown Grand Rapids, where I learned to read, is nothing compared to the confidence I gained.

Mom and I have shown true commitment. She and Dad were so proud of me and helped me through the tough times. Even when I was being stubborn and didn't want to go to tutoring for the hundred thousandth time, they encouraged me to stick with it, and I did. I think the reason that I did so well is because my parents, friends, and other family members helped me through those times, and I never truly felt alone.

That's why I am showing you the list of the people I have admired. Be sure to print out the list at www.dyslexiawonders.com. They aren't afraid to be known as dyslexics and are proud of whom they are.

As you can see, there are many important people who have dyslexia in the USA and around the world. It is of great importance that we are not saddened with the thought of being alone, because there is always someone helping us, paving the way. You may never know or recognize the person helping you get through your program. The program will teach you to learn to read and to live life.

"The question is not whether you're frightened or not, but whether you or the fear is in control. If you say, 'I won't be frightened' and then you experience fear, most likely you'll succumb to it, because you're paying attention to it. The correct thing to tell yourself is, 'If I do get frightened, I will stay in command.'"

Herbert Fenstermeim

For us, as dyslexics, the world may seem terrible and cruel. Do not lose your focus or your goal to learn. You are more important than you know. You become strong by going through things most people don't. The hardship, the struggle, and the teasing are great learning tools, which can strengthen you just by your living through it all every day. We learn that, no matter what, we are never alone despite what anyone says, and the ones we love become dearer to us with every bump in the road that we overcome.

I had to realize for myself that my reading problem was severe. This was not something I learned from being told; I had to know it from within my own self. It was extremely hard to discover that people aren't always what they appear to be. First impressions can be wrong. I had to learn the hard way, trusting the wrong people. My point is that we stand apart from the crowd—even going against it. We can do that with confidence because of the struggles that many people will never go through. It makes us stronger than those who don't have disabilities. We aren't afraid of new things or of learning that, while change can be difficult, it is well worth the journey.

> *We stand apart from the crowd—even going against it. We can do that with confidence because of the struggles that many people will never go through. It makes us stronger than those who don't have disabilities.*

One of my big journeys started when Mom and Dad told us that we were going to move. At first I thought they were joking, but when the big "for sale" sign went up, it proved that this was no joke. The next thing I remember, Mother said that we were moving in a week. My brother Brad refused to pack, and my grandma and aunt ended up packing for him. I, on the other hand, was the first to be packed. I don't think I fully understood the situation, but I packed and was ready to go. Oh, wow, to think of that day! The passing of years makes it seem almost like a dream ... but that was just the start. We lived in four different houses before the year ended. We moved into a house only to have a huge tree fall on the house unexpectedly. We were forced to move into my grandparents' house while the house was repaired. This was supposed to be for just a few months and instead it turned into a year. The house could not be repaired, so it was torn down.

We ended up spending New Year's at my grandparents', living in the basement of their house until our new house was finished being built. Moving from place to place was difficult, but overcoming my learning challenge was by far the hardest thing I have ever had to do. I have always tried to look on the bright side of things, and I keep my chin up. I am now living in a beautiful home, but the best part is in knowing that I have a family that will go to the ends of the earth to help me. That tough time brought our family closer. The journey is what life is about.

I was going through all this at the same time that I was going through my dyslexia tutoring. I tried to never complain, for I wasn't going through this alone. I had my family and friends around me and supporting me. I felt like a normal human being who just wanted to finish what she started. I love my family and hope that they know how highly I think of them. They are the foundation of who I am.

I learned from Mom to always do my best and that by always sticking with it, my own dreams will be fulfilled someday. My dear grandmother (Nana) taught me to treat others the way I want to be treated myself and that kindness is a virtue.

Each one of my family members has taught me something that I have taken to heart. The things that I have learned from them have created me. Basically, to end this never-ending speech, you are never alone. You are special and unique. If you remember that, your life will truly be the best.

"The leaders I met, whatever walk of life they were from, whatever institutions they were presiding over, always referred back to the same failure something that happened to them that was personally difficult, even traumatic, something that made them feel that desperate sense of hitting bottom – as something they thought was almost a necessity. It's as if at that moment the iron entered their soul; that moment created the resilience that leaders need."

Warren G. Bennis

Chapter 7

A Way of Life

"Thoughts lead on to purposes; purposes go forth in action; actions form habits; habits decide character; and character fixes our destiny."
Tryon Edwards

Many people wonder how to recognize dyslexia in the early stages. I know that when Mom had me checked out, I had to go to a psychologist to become officially diagnosed. Without this endorsement I was not eligible to be tutored for dyslexia at the Children's Learning Center.

The most common signs of dyslexia are:

1. Difficulty learning letter names and letter sounds
2. Difficulty with rhymes
3. Difficulty remembering rote information such as phone numbers

4. Often writing letters backwards. The most common letter written backwards is the letter *c*.
5. Difficulty with short-term memory
6. Delay in talking
7. Delay or inability in separating and correctly identifying the sounds that make up words.
8. Unable to identify rhyming words or enjoy rhymes and jingles.

These simple signs and a parent's intuition are indicators to have your child checked out for dyslexia.

After my mother was given the brush-off by my doctor and the school system, my typing teacher gave her the idea to have me diagnosed, and that was because her son was dyslexic and she recognized the symptoms. And, as you know by now, she was right on!

Your child's brain is like a sponge and is ready to learn. The earlier you get help, the less time they will need assistance. The sooner the intervention, the less a child's self-esteem is affected. Just yesterday I overheard a tutor wonder if someone would consider cleaning her house in exchange for tutoring. Two other tutors said, "Me too." I know I would have done anything to learn to read. If my parents couldn't afford tutoring I would have gladly cleaned in exchange for a reduced fee. I strongly encourage early intervention.

Sometimes the program is right in front of you, but you're the one who has to look up. You see, it is not only about knowing a program is available but what you are willing to do to help your child succeed. Don't make dyslexia the definition of who you are, but let it be simply a part of your specialness. That is the difference between a person who has it and a person who has conquered it. Because I have conquered dyslexia, I can look back without pain in my heart. My soul is stronger, and I don't regret the journey. It is just a way of life.

Because I have conquered dyslexia, I can look back without pain in my heart. My soul is stronger, and I don't regret the journey. It is just a way of life.

Chapter 8
Giving Back

"You are forgiven for your happiness and your successes only if you generously consent to share them"
William Blake, poet, artist

I will never forget the day I graduated from the Children's Learning Center. An hour before the ceremony, my family and I were all dressed up and looking pretty good when we got into the car for the hour-long drive to Grand Rapids, Michigan. Upon arrival, I was thinking that this was it, the last day I would have to step into that place as a student. Well, I was also hoping that I wouldn't make a fool of myself and trip on my heels when I went to get my diploma. But that's beside the point.

I walked in and was greeted with love and pride by people that I knew, and even some that I didn't know. I had been asked to give a speech for the occasion. My mom was also asked to do the same thing. She did the most wonderful job. She did it with such emotion that I was crying, and then it was my turn to go up and say a few words.

I was an emotional mess, but people didn't seem to care. I said thank you to the ones who helped me through it all, what a hard and wonderful journey it had been, and a few other words. After what seemed an eternity at the podium, I was applauded very loudly. I felt so happy and proud that I had done it.

The true star, I have to admit, was my mom. Even though I was the one who had dyslexia and had to go through tutoring, it was Mom who showed diligence in not giving up. She was my strength. If she had given up, I would not be writing this book—or be able to read, for that matter.

So if you are inclined to congratulate anyone, let it be her. She drove for three years twice a week to Grand Rapids, sacrificing many things just for me. That is what I call a true role model. Also, I have to give a big thank you to the Children's Learning Center for stepping up to help dyslexics. Their tutoring program is priceless—a godsend and a praiseworthy resource.

You see, there are many more people involved in this than me; I just happen to be one voice for the dyslexics. Two months after the graduation, I was able to spend fifteen minutes sharing my story in front of four thousand- four-hundred men, and was honored to do so. The organization that had invited me to speak was the Masons; it was their regional meeting. When the day came I was ready three hours early and had my speech glued to my hand because I was afraid I might lose it. My fears were unfounded, however; and not only did I not lose what I'd written, I had a wonderful time, and even received a standing ovation! Afterwards, many people had nice things to say to me.

I still can't get over the fact that I have already been able to do things in my life that others will never have the opportunity to do. It makes me realize how little time we actually have. I will continue doing my best, in the hopes of encouraging others.

It's not what problems you have; it is how you face them. Your attitude can help take a bad situation and make it better. If you truly try—and I'm not just saying for a day or two—there isn't anything you can't do. I believe that if either Mom or I had given up, I would not be where I am now.

Again, I want to say how grateful I am to The Children's Learning Center.

The program was my big chance; it gave me tools to use and people to pull for me. Now there are more kids waiting their turn to be accepted into the program. Thank you truly from the bottom to the top of my heart.

The Web site for the Children's Learning Center is http://www.childrenslearningcenters.org/.

I am now fifteen years old going on sixteen. During my freshman year I decided to attend a high school in Michigan known for its high academic standards. With great pleasure and with no hesitation I jumped right into my first school experience. I had been homeschooled my entire life. My mom  calls it home-directed since she did not teach but found other qualified teachers and classes for me to attend.

I found success early on and continue to enjoy my classes. Recently I received the honor of becoming a member of the National Honor Society. Other activities that I enjoy are singing in school, at church, and for private functions, as well as for my high school choir. I am also active in Tae Kwon Do, in which my current level is black belt, and am a certified scuba diver. Also, my team sports activities include basketball, soccer, and volleyball. At the private school, I take college preparation courses and have a high GPA, currently a 3.7. I am speaking for groups and seminars and as a keynote speaker about dyslexia and this book *Dyslexia Wonders*.

Also in the works is a new book on dyslexia tips for school success. I also promote a federal definition of dyslexia to assist children receiving the help they need regardless of which state they reside in.

Dyslexia School Tip:

Having Breakfast Changes Your Brain Having a high-protein breakfast will kick-start your brain and what you learn will stick better.

Don't feel down if a particular program doesn't work; there is one that will fit your learning style. Always keep searching. You just need to know that you can do great things. Don't let anyone tell you otherwise.

Even though life would have been easier without dyslexia, I would have missed so many things if I didn't have it. Truthfully, I'm proud to be a dyslexic and couldn't imagine not being one. I have learned life lessons that have helped me grow to the person I am and the person I am going to become.

Join me in helping to make the difference in the life of a dyslexic.

Log on to my website and follow my journey and learn how you can contribute your time, talents, and money.

"Today a reader – tomorrow a leader"
Margaret Fuller

"As long as one keeps searching, the answers come."
Joan Baez, American folks singer

Chapter 9
How Can You Help?

"I am personally convinced that one person can be a change catalyst, a 'transformer' in any situation, any organization. Such an individual is yeast that can leaven an entire loaf. It requires vision, initiative, patience, respect, persistence, courage, and faith to be a transforming leader."
Stephen R. Covey

This chapter was written by my dear mother. I hope her inspirational words will mean as much to you as they did to me.

You are your child's advocate.

Even kids with average or above-average intelligence, plenty of motivation, and ample opportunities to read can have dyslexia. Dyslexics have trouble making the connection between letters and their sounds, and they often also have difficulty with spelling, writing, and speaking. Dyslexia is often defined as a learning disability; however, it should be stressed that the condition has no effect on intelligence.

Estimates are that up to 20 percent of all people in the United States have a reading disability and that 85 percent of those people have dyslexia. Some research shows that it is inherited.

Do not rely on your school district, your doctor, or your next-door neighbor to determine whether or not your child is having trouble learning. As a parent, you know best when something is wrong with your child, so follow your instincts and keep searching until you find the right kind of help.

While certain school districts, teachers, and tutors embrace the learning-challenged, others run away—fast. Some do not use the word *dyslexia*, opting instead for the terms *reading disability* or *reading difficulty*. Most experts agree that people with dyslexia have difficulty making a connection between written words and letters and the sounds that they represent.

Some studies suggest that the condition is more common in boys than girls, while others indicate that girls can better hide their dyslexic symptoms by relying on their verbal skills. Boys, on the other hand, are more likely to be spotted at an early age as they tend to be more disruptive in school.

Rates of dyslexia are the same among all ethnic groups, but language does play a factor. For example, countries that have languages where there is a clear connection between how a word is written, and how it sounds, such as Spanish or Italian, report lower rates of dyslexia.

In spite of all the modern technology offered in schools today, few have the necessary money, space, time, faculty, or training with which to effectively deal with the diverse needs of so many children. Students with reading difficulties are often embarrassed and frustrated, and they are not going to run home and tell their parents. To them, avoidance is the key to survival—at all costs.

When I discovered that Jennifer was having trouble reading, I began reading to her out loud every day, and she followed along. I selected one *red word* (a word that does not follow the phonetic system) at a time for her to say out loud when they came up, such as *one*. After a few days, I added another word, such as *the*, still leaving the word *one* for her to read as well. Doing this task every single day with your child will reveal relatively soon whether or not your child has difficulty reading. It is not uncommon for dyslexics to have difficulties with this task.

The following tried-and-true methods, done consistently every day, will help your child remember words. I was amazed at how quickly my daughter learned once we implemented the multi-sensory technique, which utilizes the senses of sight, sound, smell, taste, and touch.

* Write the letters of a word in the air while saying each one out loud.

* Draw letters in colored sand.

* Write letters in shaving cream on the table.

* Draw letters in a pan of rice.

Not only does the dyslexic child work much harder than others in order to read, he also struggles with being bullied and teased by his peers, and maybe even members of his own family. Added to that are the burdens of believing his own parents feel he is lazy and that he has let everyone down.

If you are lucky, your school will trust your judgment and will take the proper steps to get help for your child, but don't count on it. Some parents hire an advocate to get the help that is rightfully and legally theirs.

The International Dyslexia Association (visit the Web site at www.interdys.org) offers a wealth of information about dyslexia, the research that has been done, the laws, and your rights, as well as tutoring referrals. This wonderful resource will also help you gain a solid understanding of what dyslexia is and what it is not.

Each public school child who receives special education and related services must have an Individualized Education Program (IEP). The IEP creates an opportunity for teachers, parents, school administrators, related services personnel, and students (when appropriate) to work together to improve educational results for children with disabilities. Do you have a question about an IEP? Go to www.dyslexiawonders.com to learn more about how an IEP can help ensure your child has access to the general education curriculums and what you need to know before you go.

With the proper instruction and assistance, a child with dyslexia can learn to read, thrive in school, and succeed in the workforce. But it's important for the child to be diagnosed as early as possible and to promptly get any needed support and assistance. You can receive a diagnosis as early as preschool when an assessment is done by a professional familiar with dyslexia.

It only takes one volunteer at a time to get the word out and begin making a difference. Raising awareness of dyslexia, helping individuals with their reading and writing skills, and donating money and getting others to do so as well, all add up to large community involvement.

I hope to see more volunteers come forward in the near future. Helping the dyslexics of the next generation to read and write will mean more prosperity in this great country of ours. Start getting educated about dyslexia, and include kids, who are the next up-and-coming generation that can make a difference. Bullying in our schools must stop. Many dyslexics are bullied or become bullies. By advocating help for dyslexics and insisting on early intervention, lives will be changed forever.

Individuals don't have to do huge things to make a kid happy; in fact, it's often the simplest gesture that can

turn a child around. Children are easy to please because, like us, all they want is to be understood, loved, and shown that they are loved. One of the most important things parents can do is to let their child know they believe in him or her. Don't be afraid to brag about your child, even in front of him! Let him know you are proud.

I cannot stress this enough. From one parent to another, I say to you, "Get informed and stay informed!"

Life is not always fair. Circumstances can line up in such a way as to allow you to be prejudged and convicted without a fair trial. This happens in our children's daily lives.

It may help to know that you could fight and prove your own or your child's innocence or move on and history will prove you are right.

> *"Lord grant me the serenity to accept the things I cannot change, the courage to change the things I can, and the wisdom to know the difference."*
>
> **Saint Francis of Assissi**

Choose your battles wisely. When I am faced with fighting for what is right versus accepting punishment that is unjust, even severe. I try to take a ride in a hypothetical helicopter to see the long term aerial view. Try to process your thoughts in such a way that helps you determine if the fight is worth the amount of energy and effort needed by you.

Never spin your wheels fighting a battle that even if you win, you lose. It is better to cut your losses and move on quickly. Is what you would lose critical or is it just another bump in the road? Another D paper that will soon be forgotten.

Is there another way to succeed? When one door closes another will open. When treated unfairly be sure to close the door firmly and move on to the next opportunity. This is good advice to pass on to your children but also as a way of life. Don't let the small things in life dictate for too long. Swallow the bitter medicine and move quickly to find the sweet chocolate of life.

Learn to embrace the friends that are there for you when times get tough. Let them know you appreciate their support and friendship. Try to be there for others as life occasionally knocks their legs out from under them. It is these times that create long term memories and lifelong friendships. These are the people you can truly call your friends.

> **What is easy is not always right and**
> **what is right is not always easy.**

Chapter 10

The Children's Learning Center

"Vision without action is merely a dream.
Action without vision just passes the time.
Vision with action can change the world."
Joel Barker

This chapter is written by the Director of my former tutoring center, Nina Gorak. Nina has a heart and a passion for helping kids with learning challenges. She is dedicated to helping kids who have been diagnosed with Dyslexia, tutors who help the kids learn how to read and overcome the challenges of dyslexia and to the mission of the center. Nina is a tremendous asset to the organization and a blessing to kids who have difficulty with reading.

For further information about the Learning Centers for Children, please check the website at
http://www.dyslexiawonders.com.

With my passion to help other kids with dyslexia and to help give back to the center that helped to change my world, a portion of the proceeds from every book is being donated back to the center to help other kids receive the same help I did.

You can go to the Dyslexia Wonders website to find out how you can join me in helping support this worthy cause.

http://www.dyslexiawonders.com

Nina's Inspirational Words

Jennifer's story of struggle and frustration, followed by discovery, hope, and enlightenment is at the same time unique and common. While not all children remember the hours of after-school and summer tutoring with such positive thoughts, most find the burden of schoolwork to be lessened once they complete two to three years in our program.

Jennifer, like many other children who have attended our Center, was fortunate to have a tutor with whom she bonded. Tutor Jeanne's acuity for language and her ability to instill hope, interest in learning about words, and to spark her students' determination to master the English language "monster," is a gift in itself. Teachers, even those who are not professionally trained to educate, such as parents and family or friends, may not realize what a tremendous influence they can have on a child's learning to read. Sharing the spoken and written word in a variety of forms and occasions and helping to bring it to life by relating it to one's own experiences is an unrealized resource. Creating an awareness of a word's meaning(s), its uses, and making words a fun, integral part of daily life builds a strong foundation for reading and written language.

With some basic study of child development, parents have an innate sense for when a child is struggling or avoiding certain tasks. Children who are slow in learning to talk may be at risk for dyslexia. Those children who allow others to speak for them, or who have trouble finding the right words, preferring instead to overly use general terms, such as "thing," instead of naming the object or activity, also may have difficulty learning words. Listen to your child speak. Become informed about what can be expected for oral speech at your child's age and consult with your pediatrician if you have doubts. Continue to be vigilant about listening and watching your child interact with others. When in doubt, pursue your question with a professional and be your child's advocate.

During the early school years, put your concerns in writing for school personnel and follow up, because your child most likely will not outgrow a difficulty without some intervention. Teachers and other school personnel are not always trained to recognize the symptoms of dyslexia or to provide the proper remediation. Don't give up: be persistent! As the saying goes, "better safe than sorry." Encourage testing using standardized, nationally normed materials and factual evaluations based on documented research. Keep records of all meetings and consult with professionals who have education and experience (ask them about their credentials) working with children with learning disabilities. As Anita, Jennifer's mother says, "Get informed and stay informed!"

Jennifer's story is a wonderful opportunity to tell the world about this life-changing gift currently being provided by the Scottish Rite Masons, so I am honored to contribute this information to her book.

The West Michigan Center Jennifer attended in Grand Rapids was established in 1999. Nearly 150 children and 50 teachers have received structured language training in our program. While progress is individual, just as the symptoms of dyslexia vary in severity and complexity, we are pleased to say that all children served have improved their reading, spelling, and written language skills, as well as their self-esteem, to some degree. That acclamation is necessarily vague due to the incredible range of talent and co-morbid factors, such as ADD/ADHD and depression/anxiety, affecting each child's ability to learn. Dyslexia must be the child's primary disability to qualify for the program, but cognitive, social-emotional, and instructional variances have an influence on each person's individual success. Some children make amazing gains in our program in two to three years, reaching or exceeding grade level expectations, while others would be better served by this type of instruction five days a week. In those cases, it is imperative that the child's teachers in school have this training, which unfortunately is rare: very few current university programs offer this intensive training which includes an individually supervised practicum.

The younger that children are when services begin, the more quickly they can be guided toward an understanding and functional knowledge of the alphabetic system or code. Those who are older often have a gap of several years between their age/grade and their level of expected school performance, not only due to their disability, but also as a result of being "nonreaders" for so many years. The vicious compound effect of difficulty with words, loss of self-esteem, and the understandable avoidance of tasks that are too challenging due to lack of reading/writing skills causes the mountain of problems with written language to accumulate like lava pouring from a volcano. For these children, the goal is to stop the mounting loss of chances to learn, narrow that gap, and bend the downward spiral to more of an equilibrium. Once the child realizes that she/he is capable, with greater than average effort, of learning and succeeding in school-related tasks, there is no limit to where an individual's inspiration, creativity, and natural resilience can take her/him.

Since 1994, the Learning Centers for Children have offered free tutoring to children in 15 northern states, as well as free Orton-Gillingham-based training to their teachers. At the time of this writing, there are fifty-nine 501c3 nonprofit Learning Centers from Maine to New Jersey and across to Wisconsin and Illinois. Over 7,000 children and nearly 1,500 teachers have participated in the program, but those numbers barely begin to reveal the impact of this effort. For every teacher who was trained, there are as many children with improved reading, spelling, and writing skills as each person had the ability and time to teach. And for every child whose struggle to learn was eased, there are as many families that now find life a bit brighter and the future holding many more prospects for positive contributions to society.

The program objectives of the Learning Centers for Children are to:

1) Provide, free of charge, one-to-one multisensory reading and written language tutorial services to children with dyslexia;

2) Provide, free of charge, training programs to individuals interested in becoming certified tutors in the Orton-Gillingham approach; and

3) Support research programs in dyslexia for improving clinical standards and care.

The free tutoring is funded for 34 weeks per year, 28 weeks during the academic year and 6 weeks in the summer. School-age children who have been accepted into the program attend these one-to-one individualized sessions twice a week for an hour after school and in the summer. Participants remain in the program for an average of two to three years at an estimated cost of $5,000 per child per year.

A licensed psychologist's testing for dyslexia, a specific learning disability, is required prior to enrollment in the program, and a copy of the psychological evaluation must be submitted with the program's application form. This form may be requested by contacting one of the 59 Learning Centers. The Centers have a waiting list for services, typically 6 months to a year, but possibly longer depending on the availability of tutors and the capacity of the Center. Qualified children are admitted on a first-come-first-served basis. All tutoring takes place at Center locations to allow for tutor/child supervision.

The IMSLEC [1] accredited graduate level tutor training program, using an adapted curriculum originally developed by the Learning Disabilities Unit at Massachusetts General Hospital in Boston, is conducted at each Center by certified trainers, also free of charge. The Initial Level Training requires 45 hours of classroom instruction in the Orton-Gillingham approach, and

---

1 International Multisensory Structured Language Education Council (IMSLEC), an affiliate of the International Dyslexia Association (IDA).

includes a 100-hour supervised practicum with two children at the Center. Graduate credit and Continuing Education Units (CEUs) from local universities often are available to scholars. Tutors may become paid employees once they are certified. The Centers also offer training for advanced certification, conducted over a two year period and requiring an additional 300 practicum hours.

The program's clinical protocols are built from those of the Reading Disabilities (RD) Unit at the Massachusetts General Hospital (MGH) because the Centers' Director of Training, Phyllis Meisel (currently the elected President of IMSLEC) is the former head of the MGH RD Unit. Starting in 1993, Phyllis advised the Masons in their quest to establish a new children's charity and she was appointed Clinical Director of the first Learning Center in Newtonville, Massachusetts. This Center was used as a site where some of the hospital's tutors-in-training completed their practicum. Many Learning Center Directors and tutors were trained through the MGH program.

As the number of Centers increased, a customized software program and database connecting all 59 Centers to the corporate headquarters in Lexington, Massachusetts was developed to track the children's progress and provide demographic information. Four standardized tests, the Woodcock Reading Mastery Test-Revised, the Test of Written Spelling, the Comprehensive Test of Phonological Processing, and the Test of Word Reading Efficiency are administered to each child when tutoring begins, then annually thereafter. Accumulated data is analyzed on a continuous basis to improve the program. In addition, the Director of Clinical Affairs periodically visits the Centers to observe and conduct audits in order to maintain high quality delivery of clinical services and tutor training.

For further information about the Learning Centers for Children, please check the website www.childrenslearningcenters.org, or for information about other Orton-Gillingham based programs and services for dyslexia throughout the country, check www.interdys.org and find your state's IDA branch. Some excellent books about dyslexia and the interventions needed for remediation are <u>Overcoming Dyslexia</u> by Sally Shaywitz and <u>Straight Talk About Reading</u> by Susan Hall and Louis Cook Moats. For teachers, I highly recommend Judith Birsh's book called <u>Multisensory Teaching of Basic Language Skills, 2nd edition</u>, as well as <u>Unlocking Literacy</u> by Marcia K. Henry. For help with advocacy, see www.wrightslaw.com. These are valuable starting points toward solving your child's written language and reading challenges.

<u>Reference</u>:
The IDA Commemorative Booklet from the 55th Annual Conference, "Freedom through Learning," held November 3-6, 2004 in Philadelphia, Pennsylvania.

About the Author

Jennifer Smith, leader, speaker and author of Dyslexia Wonders. She is currently in High School with a 3.7 GPA, scuba certified, black belt in Tae Kwon Do, soccer and volleyball player, singer, friend, sister and daughter.

Jennifer looks at the big picture, and knows her success is only as great as her goals. She emphasizes the possibilities rather than problems.

She wants to help others achieve this same mind-set. Jennifer keeps stretching herself, entertaining new ideas, thinking about improving herself and contemplating how to get her message of Hope & Inspiration to others.

Jennifer has overcome her difficulties by dealing with them head on, one problem at a time. She has proven herself to be a people first leader. She puts relationships and people over the task. She has a desire to help others to become inspired and to take the steps to improve their lives.

Her new project is an interview series with people who have overcome their own challenges. From medical issues, family problems, financial, spiritual or anything in between. She wants to bring stories of Hope and Inspiration to others. Share your story with Jennifer at www.StoriesOfHopeAndInspiration.com

About the Illustrator

Allison Witte, 16, Artist, member of the National Honor Society and an amazing daughter, sister, friend and classmate. Currently attends High School, where she is an outstanding art student, soccer player and choir member. Allison plans to study English and Art when she attends college. The second of four children in her family, Allison is multi-talented and enjoys art, writing, theater, staging and editing. Allison creates in a variety of mediums, has participated in several fine art workshops at Michigan State University, and has entered work in judged contests. She regularly volunteers as an editor for people that speak English as their second language. Her sense of adventure leads her to try new things.

YOUR *FREE* BONUS

The Monster File

Instant Online Access!

A guide to all the strange and mysterious
creatures that lurk in your school.

Go to

www.dyslexiawonders.com/monster

"…After Jen and I Realized That The Reason We
Got Caught Note-Passing was Because of A Little
Creature Called The 'Note-Mite', We Started
Finding More Monsters in the School. As We Found
Them I Kept Records, To Be Passed On To Future
Students. That Record is the Monster Files."

**Read and Listen to Jennifer and Allison
as they bring you the Monster File**

Claim Your Free Monster File Guide

www.dyslexiawonders.com/monster

FREE BONUS DOWNLOAD

Mind-Set For Student Success

Scientific Results Show Academic Gains When Students Participate in Self-Esteem Exercises.

Encourage your child to remember what they like about themselves and watch them build confidence, self-esteem and improve their grades. Anchor your Childs sense of self-integrity by listening to self-affirmation messages developed specifcally for Dyslexia Wonders readers.

Go to: www.dyslexiawonders.com/mindset

Also receive a Free 7 day membership to Stories of Hope and Inspiration.

BUY A SHARE OF THE FUTURE IN YOUR COMMUNITY

These certificates make great holiday, graduation and birthday gifts that can be personalized with the recipient's name. The cost of one S.H.A.R.E. or one square foot is $54.17. The personalized certificate is suitable for framing and will state the number of shares purchased and the amount of each share, as well as the recipient's name. The home that you participate in "building" will last for many years and will continue to grow in value.

Here is a sample SHARE certificate:

HABITAT FOR HUMANITY

THIS CERTIFIES THAT
YOUR NAME HERE
HAS INVESTED IN A HOME FOR A DESERVING FAMILY

1985-2005

TWENTY YEARS OF BUILDING FUTURES IN OUR
COMMUNITY ONE HOME AT A TIME

1200 SQUARE FOOT HOUSE @ $65,000 = $54.17 PER SQUARE FOOT
This certificate represents a tax-deductible donation. It has no cash value.

YES, I WOULD LIKE TO HELP!

*I support the work that Habitat for Humanity does and I want to be part of the excitement! As a donor, I will receive periodic updates on your construction activities but, more importantly, I know my gift will help a family in our community realize the dream of homeownership. **I would like to SHARE in your efforts against substandard housing in my community!** (Please print below)*

PLEASE SEND ME _____ SHARES at $54.17 EACH = $ $_____

In Honor Of: _____

Occasion: (Circle One) HOLIDAY BIRTHDAY ANNIVERSARY

OTHER: _____

Address of Recipient: _____

Gift From: _____ *Donor Address:* _____

Donor Email: _____

I AM ENCLOSING A CHECK FOR $ $_____ PAYABLE TO HABITAT FOR HUMANITY <u>OR</u> PLEASE CHARGE MY VISA OR MASTERCARD *(CIRCLE ONE)*

Card Number _____ Expiration Date: _____

Name as it appears on Credit Card _____ Charge Amount $ _____

Signature _____

Billing Address _____

Telephone # Day _____ Eve _____

PLEASE NOTE: Your contribution is tax-deductible to the fullest extent allowed by law.
Habitat for Humanity • P.O. Box 1443 • Newport News, VA 23601 • 757-596-5553
www.HelpHabitatforHumanity.org

LaVergne, TN USA
15 October 2010
200904LV00001B/6/P